BRITISH RECOVERY VEHICLES

BILL REID

AMBERLEY

Acknowledgement

The majority of the pictures in this book are from my own camera, or from my collection amassed over many years. I would like to acknowledge Pat Crang, Glen McBirnie, Alex Syme, Paul Heneachon and Ian Lawson for their assistance and permission to use their photos in the book.

First published 2019

Amberley Publishing
The Hill, Stroud
Gloucestershire, GL5 4EP

www.amberley-books.com

ISBN 978 1 4456 8215 0 (print)
ISBN 978 1 4456 8216 7 (ebook)

British Library Cataloguing in Publication Data.
A catalogue record for this book is available from the British Library.

Typesetting by Aura Technology and Software Services, India. Printed in the UK.

Introduction

Removal of vehicles for repair goes back in time well before the arrival of motorised road transport. Carts and other horse-drawn transport would break down or be damaged and needed removal for repair. At the advent of motorised transport, whether by steam, internal combustion or electricity, this type of vehicle was much heavier and presented new difficulties.

Real live horsepower would be used where the disabled vehicle could be towed on its own wheels, but in the event of accident damage occasioning missing wheels, or other important parts, the vehicle would have to be supported while being towed. Various means would evolve to allow this, and the most popular was a vehicle fitted with a crane which could partially lift and tow at the same time.

Garages and repair businesses adapted cars, or light lorries, by fitting lifting equipment at the rear that could support the front or rear end of a disabled vehicle and tow it on two wheels. As road vehicles became ever heavier, the breakdown trucks also became heavier, with a wide variation of sizes to accommodate anything from cars to heavy lorries and buses. Some of the earliest were old cars with a homemade manually operated crane. Lightweight short wheelbase lorries were fitted out in the same style.

After the Second World War, surplus military vehicles were sold off by the War Department. This allowed for much heavier breakdown trucks, sometimes based on four-wheel drive chassis, like the AEC Matador, or heavyweight 6x4 Fodens. Prior to wartime, lorries and buses had increased in size and weight, so there was a definite need for heavier recovery equipment, notwithstanding that most lorries of this time were often overladen.

In the post-war years many haulage and bus companies ran their own recovery vehicles, which were often unique and adapted for other uses, such as snowploughs or gritters, but as times changed and financial cost became a big factor in business, companies outsourced this work to recovery specialists, rather than run their own equipment manned by employees. The specialist recovery companies were able to provide a service recovering cars and heavy vehicles with purpose-built equipment, although much of it was still adapted or homemade, sometimes rather crudely.

This, in turn, saw a rise in engineering companies building bespoke recovery trucks of every size and capability. Generally, the equipment was built on time-served vehicles, but recently a move has been made to using new chassis, particularly in the heavyweight sector.

With a gradual increase in gross weight rules for heavier lorries and buses, a requirement arose for larger recovery trucks. Changing regulations governing axle weights have seen longer recovery trucks fitted with up to five axles, or with added dolly axles below the lifting point. The weight increases have brought about an increase in power and the highest manufacturer's engine power ratings are not unknown.

This book hopes to show the development of recovery vehicles from the early times to the present day and is about the vehicles, rather than their use – photographs of which I believe may engender gratuitous viewing, or feelings of grief.

Some of the earliest breakdown trucks were converted cars or light lorries. The Morris Commercial 1 tonner was well favoured as such a vehicle and this 1920s model has survived into preservation. It has a manually wound lifting crane with an A bracket to make a fixed tow. The lack of front wheel brakes must have been a disadvantage!

Similar to the Morris Commercial, the Ford AA was a small lorry often used by Ford car dealers and agents. This one, dating from 1931, has a rudimentary body, probably cut down from a larger platform, and a hand-operated crane with various adjustments apparent, which suggests it was a commercially available piece of equipment.

This is a poor picture of a recovery truck which seems to have been built by the fledgling Western SMT bus company in south-west Scotland. It is said to have had two Guy engines, presumably one for driving it and the other providing power to the lifting gear. The design seems to have been inspired by the availability of steam engine parts.

As cars and commercials became larger, there was a consequent need for heavier breakdown trucks and this fine Commer LN5 bearing a 1937 registration number seems to have been put into service as a completely new vehicle for a London Sunbeam and Talbot dealership. It has a well-engineered lifting crane, although still hand-operated, which also has a screw lift to raise or lower the jib.

The Automobile Association (AA) has always been a part of British motoring, doing roadside repairs, firstly by bicycle-mounted patrolmen, through motorcycles to larger vehicles capable of towing. The Land Rover Series 1 seen here is giving a wire rope tow to a broken-down MG sports car. This type of recovery required a good understanding between the drivers.

A 1950s Commer Superpoise 4 or 5-ton lorry which has been built as a breakdown truck, complete with a 'chariot'-style body. The lifting gear is similar to that seen on the earlier Commer LN5. The Morris Traveller being rear-end lifted looks quite new and must have given the driver and his wife serious consternation.

By the 1950s heavy lorries and buses were commonplace and when they broke down something similar was required to recover them. An ERF recovery wagon would be de rigueur for an ERF dealer, as seen here. This, probably pre-war, ERF CI has been rebuilt with a substantial lifting crane, and a small covered workshop or storage area.

In the post-war years many former military vehicles became available to the public and this Morris Commercial CS8 troop truck has been extensively altered to become a garage breakdown truck. In military use it had an open cab, or, at best, a canvas roof. It has been fitted with a lorry cab, from Commer, and a stylish chariot-style body.

Bus companies generally had more of a need for straight towing on a solid bar, and a time-expired bus from their own fleet shorn of much of its bodywork and rear overhang filled that need. The City of Portsmouth Transport Department used this Leyland Titan as a tow wagon, suitably fleet numbered T.W.2. Damaged buses could be towed using a small wheeled dolly under an axle.

A small wheeled dolly can be seen under the lifting crane on this Thames Trader of County Garage, in Carlisle, called out to a coach which has a problem. The lifting gear seems to still be hand-operated and it might be a struggle lifting the coach. The Trader itself would probably be under pressure with such a suspended tow.

24 tons gross weight was the legal maximum when this AEC Mammoth Major was running as a lorry. As a breakdown truck it would have to cope with that weight and more. It has a very substantial lifting jib, powered by hydraulic rams, to cope with heavy suspended tows. It has an RTS fibreglass cab with rear hinged doors, and may be a former Express Dairy milk tanker.

The AEC Matador was a wartime artillery tractor and it virtually became a first option for a heavy recovery truck. Most substantial bus companies used them, in various forms. They were fitted with a heavy-duty winch which made their use indispensable for many recovery jobs.

A rear view of the above AEC Matador, which was used by Birmingham City Transport, showing the lifting crane. With a safe working load of 6 tons, it would be adequate for lifting most buses of the time. An A frame towing attachment links with the lifting gear.

Dumbo is a Second World War Mack NO which has been in the ownership of Dodds of Troon since at least the 1950s. Dodds used it in its own fleet of buses and coaches and when it was part of the Ayrshire bus consortium AA Buses. The Mack was one of only a few heavy recovery trucks in south-west Scotland in the 1950s and '60s and saw frequent third party use.

A contemporary of the Mack was this Diamond T operated by Tom Carruthers in Dumfriesshire, by the busy A75 road. Carruthers had a small fleet of interesting recovery trucks, kept busy by the passing traffic on the A75 and on the main north–south A74 route.

Edinburgh Corporation Transport used this ERF CI type as a recovery truck. It has been set aside for restoration at the Scottish Bus Museum, near Dunfermline, and hopefully it will soon be seen in its original condition. The faded paint shows evidence of another livery style, possibly from when the ERF was used as a lorry.

The Leyland Martian was a 6×6 military tractor and recovery truck, powered by a large Rolls-Royce petrol engine. It was found to be lacking in suitability as a military vehicle and when sold off some became recovery trucks. Some were used with the fitted recovery gear, while others were adapted to suit. Most had the petrol engine replaced by a big diesel.

Time-expired heavy lorries were prime candidates for conversion to recovery vehicles and this early 1960s ERF KV looks to have been such a conversion. It has a well-kept appearance and is fitted with a substantial lifting crane, which would make it very capable of lifting disabled lorries or buses. The lack of a company name suggests it may have been for sale at the time of the photo. (G. McBirnie)

Car dealerships often used a recovery truck from the range of commercial vehicles that they were agents for. This well-used Austin WEK100 is a conversion of the bonneted BMC type, which the owners probably sold before taking on British Leyland marques, as seen on the livery. This type of BMC harks back through the Austin Loadstar to the 1930s-introduced Austin K Series.

This Diamond T looks as if it has come out of military service as a recovery truck. It has Holmes recovery gear with separating jibs, which can brace a pull from either side or operate as lifting gear for suspended tows. A winch drum can be seen behind the modified front bumper, which has extra lighting.

The Commer Superpoise Q4 4×4 was developed as a military truck for various uses, and for the Auxiliary Fire Service. This is a former AFS 'Bikini' truck designed for transporting firefighting equipment. Much of the AFS body has been retained and it was fitted with a rudimentary hand-operated lifting crane. The power unit was a six-cylinder 95 bhp petrol engine.

With a Liverpool-issued trade plate and painted in green, this 1930s AEC Matador is in all probability a Liverpool Corporation recovery truck. Matador was a name used by AEC for two-axle lorries before it was applied to the wartime 4x4 type. Fitted with a four-cylinder diesel engine, most were exported. A substantial Harvey Frost lifting crane is fitted.

The wartime Bedford QL 4×4 was an ex-military lorry commonly seen being put to various uses in the 1950s. This one, which has survived into preservation, is fitted with a recovery crane and a completely new body. The crane is hand-operated and would be used for car and light commercials. Access to the cab is not the best!

Another ERF KV, this one dating from 1961, carrying very substantial lifting equipment, raised by a hydraulic ram. The crane has been built very heavily with much reinforcing in the main jib, with heavy brackets elsewhere. The ERF is parked beside a 1950s Leyland Hippo, which the Crown Garage, at Tamworth, also used as a recovery truck. (G. McBirnie)

Not all it seems: at first glance this is an Atkinson Omega desert tractor chassis, but the shape of the driven front axle, the front wings and the bumper suggest otherwise. Under the Atkinson parts is a Diamond T. It was fitted with a Cummins engine by its owners, who were still using the vehicle well into the 1980s.

Another breakdown truck which has been radically altered. This Albion Chieftain began life as a tractor unit pulling a very large furniture van semi-trailer. The Albion cab was extended well beyond normal height to match the height of the trailer. It was cut down to normal height when the lorry was converted to a lightweight breakdown truck.

Preserved at the Scottish Bus Museum, this Leyland Beaver lorry would have been part of the W. Alexander bus company service fleet. The Beaver was a heavyweight Leyland lorry introduced in the 1930s and would have been very suitable for lifting and towing buses. The crane and bodywork have the look of internal skills available to a bus company.

Mason & Darlow advertise light and heavy recovery. This half-cabbed Foden must have certainly been at the heavy end! The age of the Foden is difficult to judge, but the short wheelbase suggests it may have been a tipper or dumper from the 24-ton gross era. A forklift truck counterweight has ingeniously been fitted to the front of the Foden to balance the rear lift.

The Bedford O Series as a tipper or artic unit was a prime candidate for a breakdown truck, with its compact dimensions, simple mechanicals and easy driver access. This one with a chariot-style body and handrails carries lifting gear rated for 3 tons, which is likely to be hand-operated. It has been preserved as a great example of a breakdown truck of the 1950s.

Another bus recovery truck from the former W. Alexander empire is this AEC Matador painted in the style of Fife Buses. It has had a complete body rebuild showing none of the utilitarian Matador, typical of bus company engineering. A large lifting crane has been fitted. It was seen attending a bus event at the Scottish Bus Museum, at Lathalmond, near Dunfermline.

The bonneted Leyland Comet was a popular lorry developed in the late 1940s, and found many uses in transport and industry. This one was used initially as an artic unit by Armstrong Whitworth Aviation, then became a recovery truck in the colours of the later British Aerospace. It has since been returned to artic unit form, pulling a restored livestock semi-trailer.

The large engineering department of Western SMT Buses was capable of turning out all types of work, and their tow wagons were something to behold. This greatly modified AEC Matador probably has only the original chassis and axles, as a Gardner 6LXB engine was fitted. The bodywork has been finished with a half cab reminiscent of old single-deck buses.

A Scammell Explorer 6×6 military truck on display at the British Commercial Vehicle Museum. For all its size the lifting gear fitted was rated at 3 tons, but the vehicle had the capability of going almost anywhere, such was the suspension articulation. Some had Meadows engines, while others were fitted with Gardner or Rolls-Royce diesels.

The London Brick Company had a very large fleet of delivery lorries, mainly of AEC manufacture, in the 1950s and '60s, and when a tow truck was required it was natural to use a time-expired AEC. This one, a Mercury, has no lifting gear and would be used as a solid drawbar tow truck. It has ballast weight over the rear axle to give the tyres some grip.

Found in a yard near Kilmarnock, Ayrshire, this old Thames Trader dated from 1963. It was never ascertained if it was used as a breakdown truck, or if it was an ongoing project.

As already mentioned, bus companies had the skills to turn out whatever they required. South Yorkshire Transport had this Leyland Titan double-decker very neatly converted to a solid bar tow wagon. The Leyland would have been one of the last front-engined double-deckers to go into service, in 1964.

A fully restored Diamond T recovery unit built during the Second World War. It is fitted with Holmes recovery gear, which may be a more modern equivalent of the original equipment. The long bonnet and small cab are very characteristic of American trucks of the time, and set the style for the so-called 'conventional' US trucks of today.

This Foden S20 may have originally been built as a mobile drilling rig, with a much longer wheelbase. The crew cab is unusual, with the front suspension exposed, as in pictures seen of the drilling rig. It has a heavy hydraulically lifted crane and relatively compact dimensions. It had been entered in a Donnington vintage vehicle sale at the time of the photograph.

Another re-engineered bus, this time a Bristol K which has been stripped to the chassis and rebuilt using newer bus body parts. As a bus it would have had an exposed radiator, and in rebuild has been given the style of the later Bristol Lodekka. It is simply a solid bar tow wagon. (G. McBirnie)

This rear view shows the towing attachment and the rear end of the body, which probably doubled as a transport lorry. The vehicle is lettered to the Bournemouth Transport Museum, which is housed in a bus garage on the edge of the town. (G. McBirnie)

Another radical conversion. Under the Volvo F88 cab is an Albion WD.FT11, which is the Albion version of the Second World War 3-ton 4×4 general service army truck. In this instance the replacement cab is badly needing replacement too. It is not known if the vehicle was restored to original condition. It is believed to have been a bus company tow wagon.

The BMC Austin Gypsy was intended as competition to the ubiquitous Land Rover, but it did not compete in sales due to several factors. This is a particularly well restored example fitted with light car-type lifting equipment and would have been a garage hack, as depicted here.

Again, a short wheelbase artic unit was considered a good base for a recovery truck, and this 1964 Atkinson Silver Knight was ideal. By the later 1960s it would be obsolete as an artic unit, with its Gardner 6LX 150 bhp engine and 24-ton gross train weight.

This BMC FGK300 was originally a bread delivery van, until it was converted to a lightweight breakdown truck. With its lightweight hand-operated lifting crane it would have been ideal for car recovery in the Lanarkshire Clyde Valley, where it was based. It is in preservation now, and a regular participant in the Ayrshire Road Run.

Another of the former Western SMT recovery trucks was this big AEC Militant 6×6. Much modified by the Western engineers, it operated from the Dumfries bus garage, where it survived into preservation. It was a slow and steady piece of equipment with a Harvey Frost heavy lifting crane counterbalanced by the spare wheel.

The National Coal Board had a large fleet of lorries, with depots around the major coalfields. This 1958 Leyland Beaver would have been a tipper in the fleet before becoming the recovery truck at the Prestwick maintenance depot. (A. Syme)

Kerr & Smith of Cumnock, Ayrshire, is a car and commercial dealer and this Diamond T was one of its early recovery trucks. It is fitted with the older style Holmes lifting gear and has an enclosed cab in lieu of a possible open-top military type. The lifting gear was later temporarily fitted to a much more modern AWD TM 6×6.

The Basset Group is a well-known transport company in the Midlands. Long ago, they put an ex-army Foden DG6 into use as a recovery truck, and over the years it was modified and updated to the form seen here. The lifting gear does not look very substantial but calibration marks show it could lift 6 tons.

Another radical conversion: a Leyland Martian chassis and the military lifting gear as supplied, with a Scania 111 cab and a Scania engine fitted. Unfortunately, it was too slow for practical purposes and was later dismantled.

This type of Seddon, possibly a 14:4:370, with a Leyland engine, was not a common sight as a recovery truck. This rather rudimentary example was attending a Tyne–Tees Road Run quite a number of years ago. It has hydraulic lifting gear fitted, and a set of Bedford KM bumpers.

An LV-cabbed ERF, which may have been a heavy haulage tractor. It has been fitted with a heavy lifting crane and a bespoke equipment box, all finished in a new paint job, as if the vehicle had recently gone into service. Denny Tippers is a large haulage company operating in central Scotland.

The Austin K9 military 4×4 truck was a favourite with small garage businesses as a breakdown truck. This is a more modern version with the BMC-style cab front panels, but it is essentially the same. The lifting gear, obscured by the owner, appears to be quite substantial for such a small truck.

This Atkinson recovery truck was on display at the CVRTC show at Crick in the early '90s. The lifting gear appears to be unfinished, with no winch cable evident. A PTO handle is visible in the cab, suggesting hydraulic lifting action.

A Foden S21-cabbed six-wheeler recovery truck looking in absolutely pristine condition. It is not known if it was finished as a show truck, or if it went into use. The small grille panel below the Foden 'kite' was a modification fitted to concrete mixer chassis to allow extra cooling. An extended and ballasted front bumper has been fitted to compensate for the short wheelbase.

Greater Manchester Buses was, like most bus companies, adept at bodywork and mechanical engineering, and when it modified its AEC Matador tow truck it used window glass and panels common to many of its buses in service. The end result has given a much more modern look to the very utilitarian wartime vehicle.

The owner of this Scammell Highwayman built the hydraulic lifting gear himself using a lorry chassis and his metalworking skills. He advertised a 23½-hour service as he said everybody needs half an hour to do what everybody needs to do every day! The Scammell has since moved into the world of preservation as a showman's tractor.

Once a lorry in the ownership of Kevin Dennis from Skegness, at the time of the photo this vehicle had found its way to Scotland and was in a rally for Rootes-made vehicles in the hands of Dennis (Ben) Gunn from Edinburgh. It has a Harvey Frost crane, but whether it is a true Commer Maxiload is open to conjecture.

Glen Harley's eight-wheel recovery truck, with another on a suspended tow. The eight-wheeler is not all it seems as underneath the Leyland cab is an AEC Mammoth Major Mk 5. It has been in use at Hudson's Garage in south Cumbria for years. Glen Harley is on the far left of the picture.

Another eight-wheeler, in this instance a 1966 Cummins-engined Atkinson Black Knight, which has been converted into a very tidy recovery vehicle. John Glass, of Kilbirnie, was the owner at the time of the photo. The Atkinson has since been returned to tipper form and became part of the Donald Malcolm heritage fleet of restored vehicles.

Barr Construction was a well-known civil engineering company in Scotland. Among its equipment was this Magirus Deutz 6x6 heavy tractor. While it was not fitted with lifting equipment, its pulling and winching power was prodigious. (A. Syme)

Another tow truck without lifting gear was this 1968 Leyland Beaver, which had originally been an artic unit. With its very short wheelbase, it would be quite manoeuvrable in busy town or city traffic, making it an ideal bus company tow wagon.

An ERF from the 1960s bearing a Q plate, making its age indeterminable. It has been kept in working order by D. A. Roberts, with no aspirations of being a show truck, although it was taking part in a recovery vehicle rally held at Leyland's British Commercial Vehicle Museum in the 1990s when seen.

From around the same era as the Roberts ERF, this former 1974 Seddon 32:4 artic unit had been run by SRS Engineering (part of British Road Services) as a recovery truck. The short wheelbase and the light hand-operated lifting gear might not have been ideal in the 32–38-ton era.

This 1970 Leyland Retriever with its long wheelbase would have been a better counterbalance for its crane. It has been fitted with a substantial lifting frame. The Leyland Retriever was a lighter six-wheeler introduced at a time when articulation was allowing heavier weights. It did not enjoy a great success against even lighter six-wheel Leyland chassis.

Barry Devlin is a major recovery operator in the west of Scotland. This Foden S39 was an early heavy recovery truck in the fleet, fitted with home-built hydraulic lifting equipment. The Foden, fitted with a Gardner engine, served well on the Ayrshire roads. It is pictured here in its latter days, in a well-worn condition but still useful.

The last of the military AEC Militant 6×6 recovery units were well sought after by civilian operators. This one, operated by the long gone Seaplane Motors of Prestwick, was just about to tow away a damaged bus on a solid bar. A characteristic of the Militant when suspended towing was to sit down on the rear springs, relieving the front axle of weight and positive steering.

Another former artic unit converted to a recovery truck was this 1967 ERF 64G. The Gardner badge says it has a 6LXB engine, which would provide good pulling power, but the short wheelbase must have compromised lifting ability. It is in preservation and is regularly seen at Scottish vintage events.

At the start point of a TransPennine Road Run in the late 1980s or early '90s is this Foden S21 in the style and livery of Ripponden & District Parcel Carriers. The long wheelbase allows for an enclosed workspace and good counterbalance for the lifting equipment. The cab is Foden's first fibreglass type, sometimes known by the nicknames of Sputnik or Mickey Mouse.

Ronnie Devlin of Tourhill Commercials was to introduce this bonneted Scania 111 into his fleet, which proved to be a useful piece of equipment. It is fitted with Swedish EKA recovery equipment enclosed in a neat body. Underlift gear was fitted so that it could raise buses and coaches on their wheels. It is seen waiting to recover an articulated tipper which had left the road.

The other side of Swedish truck manufacture is highlighted by this 1977 Volvo F86. It also has underlift spectacle equipment, more suited to lighter recovery than the EKA-equipped Scania. The registration number suggests the Volvo may have come from the well-known W. H. Malcolm fleet.

In the 'Fair City of Perth', also known as the Gateway to the Highlands, Frews was the local Ford dealership, and to promote the marque it used a middleweight Ford D Series with Holmes 800 lifting equipment. The age of the truck is not apparent, but the eye-catching livery certainly is!

This is a 1966 AEC Majestic, part of a range of export chassis developed by AEC in the 1960s. This one was not exported and became a recovery truck, last used by Lex Tillotson at Wrexham, after which it passed to preservation ownership. It has the AEC AV760 engine.

A real heavyweight and a former heavy haulage locomotive operated by Pickfords from their Glasgow depot, which Allan Syme of Newtyle, Dundee, rebuilt as a recovery truck. It carries a rotating crane, which appears to have been sourced from a Leyland Martian, and carries a Bedford TM cab in place of the Scammell original.

Shelvoke & Drewry was always associated with refuse collectors. This is a TN type, which was designed as a short and narrow vehicle to access side streets and alleys. It was converted to a recovery truck, working for a scrap dealer. It would be able to access many places bigger recovery trucks could not get to.

The Atkinson Defender was a long-lived articulated unit, seeing service in many large fleets. Thomas Graham, a builder's merchant, kept this 1972 model in Glasgow to deal with breakdowns across their fleet. It has since been restored to tractor unit form by J. & M. Murdoch of Neilston.

Howie of Dunlop, in Ayrshire, was once a large agricultural and timber merchant with a varied fleet of lorries serving the farming community. In the 1990s it operated this 1972 Bedford MK 4×4 recovery truck. It was extensively altered for recovery and could be fitted with a heavy snowplough for snow clearance in and around the Howie milling properties.

The former Scottish Bus Group companies had a great engineering heritage and made their own bespoke tow wagons. This one, a 1972 Leyland Leopard, originally a single-deck bus with a W. Alexander Y type body that was new to Western SMT, became a standardised SBG tow wagon with Highland Buses.

Small garages still had a need for light recovery trucks when A. G. Peters of Troon was running his small Ford D Series, which could lift disabled vehicles or transport new or used cars. It is not in concours condition by any means, but would be a useful tool within the owner's business.

A 66Cu ERF of 1968 with the LV cab and fitted with Holmes-type recovery equipment on display at a CVRTC show in the old BP Crickstop in in the early 1990s. Through the mist of time, it can't be recalled which of the names was the actual operator. Crouch has a formidable recovery fleet in the present day.

Scammell's Trunker artic unit was seen as a good compact recovery chassis. McCall's Coaches of Lockerbie, in southern Scotland, had this one, which appears to have been lengthened, perhaps to give some counterbalance to the lifting gear. It is seen displayed at the annual Biggar Vintage Rally.

The Dodge K Series was one of the first British lorries to be fitted with a V8 diesel. It was a popular type because of the cab size and proven running gear. This 1970 double drive type has been converted to a recovery unit on a compact wheelbase and fitted with heavily engineered lifting gear. The engine is a Cummins V8, and has a wonderful bark when being driven hard.

Operated from the Cumbrian Fells railway town of Tebay for many years was this 1968 Volvo FB88. It is fitted with Wreck Master equipment and would have been well placed for use on the adjacent M6, which is often prone to bad weather. It is in tidy condition, befitting a hard-worked vehicle.

Ashfield Motors was a recovery company which operated from Glasgow some years ago. It had heavy recovery trucks and this Bedford TJ Packhorse 4X4 for air-bag recovery. It is parked beside the ubiquitous Diamond T heavy recovery truck which Ashfield also used.

Another Ford D Series, but closer to the end of production. This one, built as a 'sloper', has a hydraulic loading crane which would enable it to lift on and off accident-damaged cars, allowing a much easier and safer method of recovering severely damaged vehicles.

Not all bus company tow wagons were former buses. Lowland Scottish had this 1972 Guy Big J lorry rebuilt to tow buses in the Scottish Borders. It has been painted to the usual bus industry traditions and was on show at the old Scottish Bus Museum near Whitburn in the early 1990s.

Killingbeck Transport was a company well known for its specially altered Atkinsons. Its recovery truck was one of these specials. Fitted with a forklift mast, it could unload trailers before recovery, although what it was like to manoeuvre is another question.

W. H. Malcolm had this Mack as a recovery truck and made good use of it, until it was sold to Dallas Recovery of Glasgow. In time it returned to Malcolm's and was restored, becoming part of the Donald Malcolm heritage fleet. From experience, the cab is very small and cramped! (P. Heneachon)

The Ford Transit was used as a light recovery truck by many small garages across the country. This 1978 version, with a third axle, was about to recover a broken-down car. The third axle was simply a dead drive axle, with uncompensated semi-elliptical leaf springs. The ruin to the rear is Crossraguel Abbey, a well-known Ayrshire landmark.

A 1980 Foden S10 which looks as if it has been a tipper in a previous life. Fitted with a TFL crane, it was operated from Lesmahagow, near the top end of the A74, later the M74, and was well used, as its condition shows. The view to the right of the Foden is where the new Route 74 Truckstop is built.

Everybody knows of the Egertons Recovery Service, if only from seeing its recovery vehicles on the motorways and in service stations. The large fleet has contained many different types, and this Scammell Crusader with Century lifting gear, which was for a time based at Southwaite Services on the M6, epitomises the equipment on standby.

The Fire and Rescue Service had recovery vehicles, depending on individual brigade needs. The London Fire Brigade used this heavy 1963 Dennis with Harvey Frost lifting gear. It has been preserved.

Seen at a vintage rally in Dalkeith, this is a former Department of Transport Atkinson 6×6 gritting lorry, which was used on the UK motorways and trunk roads. The lifting gear is capable of bracing and pulling from either side, as well as over the rear.

Not the most common recovery truck type: this is a Russian Ural 4320 truck imported by a small garage in southern Scotland. The garage proprietor, Mr W. Bone, equipped this one with Holmes-type lifting gear for his own use. Engines available were 11-litre V6 or 14.9-litre V8 diesels.

The recovery business of G. Mutch was based in Perth. It operated this fine Magirus Deutz bonneted recovery truck, seen here parading at a Scottish Truckfest. The recovery gear seems to be hydraulic and cable-operated, capable of lifting and towing any challenge on the nearby A9 road to the north of Scotland.

A small recovery truck based on a light GMC truck chassis. The recovery gear does not look very heavy and was probably used on car breakdowns and recovery. GMC trucks were not imported into the UK for sale, and it may have been acquired as a US military surplus vehicle.

A very fine example of a 1979 ERF B Series lorry that has been converted to a tidy, well-kept recovery unit, and which was used in the early 1990s by B&S of Leyland. It was photographed at a recovery vehicle show held in Leyland in the early 1990s.

Lynx Parcels was a big combine that replaced BRS Parcels across the country. This 1974 Atkinson Borderer was extended and converted to a recovery unit. It seems to have been the 'pet' recovery truck as it was always turned out for shows in immaculate condition. It was later returned to being a platform lorry in green BRS Parcels livery, solely as a show truck.

Dodge Commandos, née Commer, were relatively rare as recovery units. George Fuller of Ayr had this one, a G1075 which he used on the local police rota system when not going about his business as a motor engineer.

A Scammell Trunker of 1970 with a Harvey Frost crane which was operated by Citybus in Lancashire about twenty-five years ago. It is not a pristine vehicle by any means, and looks as if it has been working normally up to the day of the photograph.

The Ford Cargo was the successor to the Ford D Series lorry and came to be equally well liked. This example operated by South Scotland Coachworks near the M74 has spectacle lifting gear and was probably used for lighter breakdowns and recovery. Spending much time parked in the harsh hill weather at Elvanfoot has taken its toll on the paintwork.

Dallas Recovery was another Glasgow recovery operator. Its Atkinson Viewline was seen parked in Bothwell Services, perhaps as an immediate recovery vehicle for the interminable roadworks on the motorway at the time. The Viewline was an attempt by Atkinson to market a high cab, but its construction was not durable. They were uncomfortable in hot and cold weather.

A recovery in action on the M74 south of Hamilton. The Volvo FB88 is running under the two company names of W&J Riding, whose Seddon-Atkinson is being recovered, and McIntyre & Elder Motors. Riding was absorbed by the Transport Development Group and lost its identity. McIntyre & Elder may have been a Riding subsidiary, which is still trading.

Another of the Scottish Bus Group standardised tow wagons on a 1965 Leyland Leopard chassis, which is a former Western SMT bus. In this instance it has been painted in the Stagecoach corporate livery of the time, soon after the Western takeover.

Remaining with a bus theme, this 1984 MAN long wheelbase six-wheeler was used by Jackie Dunsmore in his business of bus breaking, hence the fitting of heavy lifting gear capable of going under long front overhangs. The reflective lining, picked out by the camera flash, round the cab and along the body sides would be very effective in headlamps at night.

Baldoukie Motors of Forfar in east Scotland had this big DAF fitted with Holmes lifting gear. It is likely to have been a heavy haulage tractor in a former use, but the power ratings have been removed. It could be anything from a 2800, through 3300 to a 3600 rated for 100 tons plus.

If this Atkinson looks a little strange it is because it was originally fitted with a Viewline cab, as seen earlier in the book. The Viewline front axle was closer to the front of the chassis, which has resulted in this rather odd look after fitting a normal Atkinson cab. It probably didn't detract much from the purpose the vehicle was intended for.

With the introduction of more modern Foden chassis into military service, many 6x4 Scammell Crusader artic units became available to civilian buyers. Peacock of Dumfries, Leyland DAF dealers, had this ex-military Scammell as part of its recovery fleet. The lifting gear incorporates a heavy winch behind the cab. Note the concrete bumper counterbalance!

MJ Auto & Commercial operates in the south of England. Its very smart Scania 93 was seen at the 2007 Southwest Truckfest in resplendent condition. Holmes-type lifting gear is fitted, but with only 230 bhp it might not have been used for heavy lifts. (P. Crang)

An Atkinson Searcher which may have served as a heavy haulage artic unit is seen arriving at the Leyland Museum with another Atkinson on suspended tow. A heavy winch is fitted to the lifting jib. The late Billy Littlejohn, well known in Scottish lorry circles, looks on.

James Willingham of Thorngumbold, near Hull, was a recovery operator and builder of recovery trucks. This 1985 Leyland Freighter is one of his lighter slide back units awaiting the call to work at his base and workshop beside the River Humber.

A larger recovery unit in the South Scotland Coachworks fleet in the shape of a Volvo F10 with a lifting rear axle. The recovery gear had a long underlift arm to cope with front overhangs. The SSC base overlooks the M74 south of Crawford and Abington.

This Tourhill Commercials G Series Renault awaits a discussion about how a rather difficult recovery of a large laden artic would take place. The Renault is fitted with Interstater recovery equipment, giving a low-profile look to the vehicle.

Due to the sturdiness of the chassis and the generally rot-free cab construction, the Atkinson had a long life and good reputation, usually in preservation. This 1970 example, fitted with a Harvey Frost crane and a bespoke body, has been around for a long time. Depending on how you see it, this one could be a Silver Knight or a Borderer, in Atkinson terminology.

Like the Scottish Bus Group, the bus company Yorkshire Traction modified one of its 1970 Leyland Leopard buses to make a tow wagon. The Alexander body has been cut down, leaving some crew accommodation, while the rear has been rebuilt with a useful cargo body.

Very similar to the Tourhill Commercials Scania 110, this one dating from 1971 also has Swedish EKA recovery equipment fitted with neat locker installation in the EKA style. A heavy front bumper has been fitted, which appears to have snowplough attachments.

Alexander Latto operates recovery vehicles in the Edinburgh area. Its large Scammell Crusader is one of 130 ordered for the British Army in 1977. They had EKA recovery equipment, rated for a 16-ton lift, while the vehicle had a nominal military 30-ton towing capacity.

The Tyne–Tees Road Run has long been a favourite in the vintage events calendar. Like other road runs, a recovery truck usually took part in case of breakdowns. This fine Volvo F88 operated by Dowse Crane Hire, capable of air cushion recovery, took part in the 1990s and is seen at the end of the event in South Shields.

Fleetcare of Airdrie, in central Scotland, had this 1986 Seddon-Atkinson artic unit converted to a short wheelbase recovery truck. It was kept in good order and invariably parked outside the premises beside the busy A73 road as a sort of advert for Fleetcare services.

A DAF six-wheel chassis converted to a recovery truck, with Holmes lifting gear. Bearing a Q plate, the vehicle may be a mixture of parts. The sleeper cab is from the lighter DAF range of artic and rigid trucks, while the chassis and engine may be heavy haulage equipment. No clues to the engine power rating are fitted.

Lothian Regional Transport, formerly Edinburgh Corporation Transport, had this Leyland Roadtrain with Crane Freuhauf recovery equipment. It is seen in Edinburgh's Princes Street in a traffic jam long before the coming of the new trams. (Author's collection)

A fine Volvo F12 in the service of TT Breakdowns, with neat bodywork surrounding underlift recovery gear. The occasion was a show for recovery trucks at the British Commercial Vehicle Museum in Leyland in about 1993.

MTS Recovery of Perth had this Scania 143 on the books, with underlift equipment on a long wheelbase chassis compensated by a ballasted front bumper. It is seen at a Scottish Truckfest some years ago.

A good looking ERF B Series recovery truck operated by BVT, or Blackpool Van Transport. Again fitted with a long reach underlift system, this outfit represents the state-of-the-art recovery truck of the 1990s.

An alternative to recovering broken down buses and coaches over long distances was the lowloader trailer developed for the purpose. N. L. Walling of Preston used this early version, which allowed long overhang vehicles to be loaded damage-free. Here, the trailer is pulled by a Leyland DAF 95. It was later used with a Renault Magnum, which was impressive with a recovered coach.

The Craig Dymock business operates in central Scotland and has an impressive line-up of recovery trucks. This Leyland Constructor slide back lorry with a heavy loading crane and spectacle lifting equipment would have been a handy vehicle in the fleet.

Robert Campbell Commercials is primarily a breaker of commercial vehicles and this 1987 Volvo F10 recovery truck would have been busy towing in such vehicles for scrapping. Underlift equipment is fitted, with a heavily tyred rear tag axle. Robert Campbell has an impressive collection of vintage vehicles often seen around the Scottish vintage shows.

Another former military Scammell Crusader with the Swedish EKA recovery equipment. This one, with an extended, probably ballasted front end with a winch gear, operated for Armstrong Transport Services of Cumbria, which had its own fleet of lorries.

One of the most impressive recovery trucks in the south of Scotland was this Diamond REO, operated by Gateside Commercials, a Dodge dealership in Dumfries. The Wreck Master recovery gear has similarities to the better known Holmes equipment, and operated on the same principles. Diamond REO was a short-lived name in US truck history.

Greater Manchester Buses used this Mercedes-Benz 1735 for bus recovery and possibly third party work. It is a former artic unit given a very long wheelbase extension and has been fitted with a pusher axle ahead of the driving axle for increased load capacity and stability.

The Leyland Roadtrain was the last new Leyland heavy artic unit, and was superseded after the DAF takeover by the DAF 95. Roadtrains were then good candidates for conversion to recovery trucks, and Robinson's of Bolton had this one tidily converted, with a wheelbase extension.

ERF lorries are another long-lasting type with their strong chassis and fibreglass panelled cabs. MC Recovery had this eight-wheeler converted, probably from a tipper chassis, with Holmes lifting gear. It has been adorned with a patriotic Scottish livery.

Forsyth of Denny fitted this Seddon-Atkinson with double boom lifting gear. The rear axle looks more widely spaced than standard, and may be an added tag axle. Forsyth is still engaged in crane hire haulage.

Probably an ex-military tractor unit, judging by the Q registration plate, this Scammell Crusader has been given a chassis extension and has been fitted with bespoke type underlift equipment. When supplied to the military these lorries were badged as Leylands. JSM is well placed in Bury for the motorways surrounding Manchester.

Thomas Ash is a well-known Glasgow recovery operator of long standing. Its Scania 112, on show at an early Scottish Truckfest near Edinburgh, is extolling the virtue of being Scotland's heaviest underlift at the time.

Barry Devlin Services expanded over the years and has had some interesting equipment. Its Volvo FL10 with underlift gear is about to uplift a police vehicle which had broken down on an LGV training course. The Volvo carries the same colours Barry Devlin set out in business with.

A picture of the difference in lorry sizes. The Seddon-Atkinson dwarfs the lightweight Bedford TK, which is fitted with spectacle recovery equipment and a cable-equipped crane. It is thought both vehicles are operated by the same company. The black paint job is uncharacteristic of recovery vehicles, where their normally bright colours are a great factor in road safety.

This was Ian Gordon's first recovery truck, based on a MAN artic unit. It is fitted with James Willingham-built recovery gear and bodywork, with an underlift arm and rear stiff legs. It was later modified to have an extended ballasted bumper.

Millers of Longton is a well known Lancashire recovery operator. Some of its recovery trucks were much modified from the original and this Leyland/Scammell is no exception. It is believed to have been a three-axle heavy haulage unit when acquired by Millers.

An early Volvo F10 with underlift equipment operated by Baldoukie Motors not far from the A90 Aberdeen–Dundee road, where it would see plenty of activity. It has the air of a working vehicle, although it is seen on display at a vintage event held in the grounds of Scone Palace, near Perth.

The M8 Recovery flagship: a highly detailed Peterbilt with imported underlift gear. It is very American, with twin upright exhaust pipes and lots of chrome bling. The comment on the fly deflector is a humorous reference to another Glasgow recovery operator.

Some recovery operators like to have versatility in their vehicles. This Foden 4375 is a tag axle artic unit with the recovery equipment fitted to a fifth wheel dolly, which can be detached when the need arises to use the Foden as it was originally intended.

The lightweight IVECO Fiat 7.5-ton wasn't often seen as a recovery truck. An Ayrshire garage, J. K. Thomson of Cumnock, used this one as a recovery truck and transporter mainly for its customers and as part of a police recovery rota.

Ashfield Motors had a variety of recovery vehicles, as seen here. The largest was this Scania 141 with underlift equipment, and it was well supported by lightweights such as the Fords in the background. There was also a Foden S39 eight-wheeler. The sight of the Foden and the Scania double-heading a very large multi-axle mobile crane on a rigid tow was something to behold!

The normally export ERF MW was an uncommon sight in the UK. In this instance we see two of Beresford Transport's small fleet of them. The song lyric 'He ain't heavy, he's my brother' comes to mind! The cab fitted to the ERF MW models was a variation of the Motor Panels cab seen on various other chassis makes.

Another of Glasgow's recovery operators is 911 Recovery, which has blossomed in recent times from lightweight recovery to heavy truck and bus work. Its MAN TG-X, photographed when fairly new, shows off the livery style used from the start, which certainly catches the eye. (P. Heneachon)

A compact recovery unit based on a Seddon-Atkinson Strato in use with Blue Line Coaches of South Wales, which had driven up to Scotland to take part in a Scottish Truckfest a few years ago. The cab is a lighter and simplified version of the Cab-Tech design seen on other S-A trucks, and DAFs.

The owners of M8 Recovery can never be referred to as shrinking violets as far as publicity is concerned. For their lighter recovery vehicles some US trucks were imported, and this 2006 International is something different in the UK recovery scene. Fitted with underlift and a crane, it would be a versatile truck.

The Renault, née Berliet, R range was an uncommon type in recovery. This R365 artic unit has been made into an attractive recovery truck with underlift gear for JDS Recovery in Lancashire.

The Scammell S26 was intended as a heavy-duty lorry, mainly for export at higher weights than permitted in the UK, or as a heavy haulage unit. It was one of the last Scammell designs and used the Leyland T45 range cab in its largest form. Previously owned by G. Mutch of Perth, it has passed into CRS (Chisholm) ownership.

Autotech of Port Glasgow ran this large Scania 164 fitted with an underlift, which is seen demonstrating its abilities by giving another Autotech truck a rear end lift. Well balanced, the Scania hardly noticed the weight of the lift.

The Scottish Truckfests were good events at which to see a variety of recovery equipment. Nottingham Autocraft brought its Volvo F10 with twin-boom recovery gear, with functional bodywork and a ballasted front bumper.

Ward's of Burnley is a well-known Lancashire recovery business with a range of recovery trucks covering all eventualities. This one, from the originally imported MAN range, may have been a heavy haulage tractor, or perhaps a 30-ton eight-wheeler with the second axle removed. At that time MAN did not market a three-axle chassis in the UK.

As has been mentioned before, some of the longer distance road run events had a modern recovery truck travelling with the vintage entrants. Highway Recovery sent this Scania 93 to a TransPennine Run in the 1990s, which would have been well capable of dealing with any mishaps across the Pennines.

Barry Devlin Services, like many other recovery operators, acquired this former military Foden 6x6. More than 330 of these Fodens were received by the military in the mid-1980s. Fitted with EKA recovery equipment, they were intended as replacements for Scammell Crusaders.

A late ERF B Series artic unit converted to operate as a recovery truck in Lancashire with underlift equipment. It has a tidy body and well-finished livery.

A brand new Foden 4350 for Kirkcaldy Council on display at the Scottish motor racing circuit at Knockhill in 1989. Fitted with a spectacle lift for any type of council vehicle, it apparently did not find favour and became part of the Stuart Dymock fleet in central Scotland.

A very rare Zeligson, particularly as a recovery truck. Zeligson began as a producer of refurbished war-surplus trucks. Many special types were produced before production closed in 1989. Allan Syme, of Newtyle Commercials, used this Cummins-powered version as a heavy-duty recovery truck.

Going back to more conventional recovery trucks, this DAF 85CF has been in service with NORSCOT Truck & Van, the Aberdeen DAF dealership, for a good number of years. Fitted with twin-boom lifting gear, it looks in excellent condition. It has been named *Bulldog*.

Attending a CVRTC Show at the former BP Truckstop near Crick in 1991 was this Scania 141 with the ubiquitous Holmes twin-boom lifting gear. It was well turned out and a great advertisement for the operator. It was operated from the English village of Moira in Leicestershire, rather than the similarly named Moira in Northern Ireland.

An old Seddon-Atkinson of indeterminate age which was operated by Southern Scottish Coachworks when they were based in the village of Crawford, beside the M74. It would have seen considerable action on this hilly part of the M74, often blighted by bad weather.

On a very windy day in the East Midlands this large Peterbilt conventional had been sent out to recover the attached Volvo, which may have been blown over. Fitted with American Jerr Dan recovery gear and a neat body, this was apparently the Peterbilt's first job in the UK.

The last ERF type was the ECX, which could be specified with the Olympic sleeper cab. Such a cab is fitted to this Brooks Auto Services ERF, which has been converted to a lifting recovery unit. It appears to have a demountable dolly axle for the underlift gear. (P. Crang)

Preston Bus had this tidy Seddon-Atkinson Strato with underlift equipment and a 400 bhp engine, which was in all probability a Cummins. The bodywork is well matched to the boxy shape of the Cab-Tech cab.

One of Kerr & Smith's 410 bhp IVECO Trakker recovery trucks. It was accompanying an Ayrshire Road Run a few years ago when seen. Pleasingly, its capabilities were not required.

Mollinsburn is a village between Glasgow and Cumbernauld beside the A80/M80. Kane's EKA-equipped Scania 112 would have plenty of call outs on that road. It is finished in a tidy style with plenty of yellow for visibility.

Another road run 'sweeper'. This Volvo FL10 was the official breakdown wagon on a Tyne–Tees Road Run some years ago. It is seen in the Gypsy's Green Stadium at South Shields. The owners were enthusiastic vintage vehicle restorers.

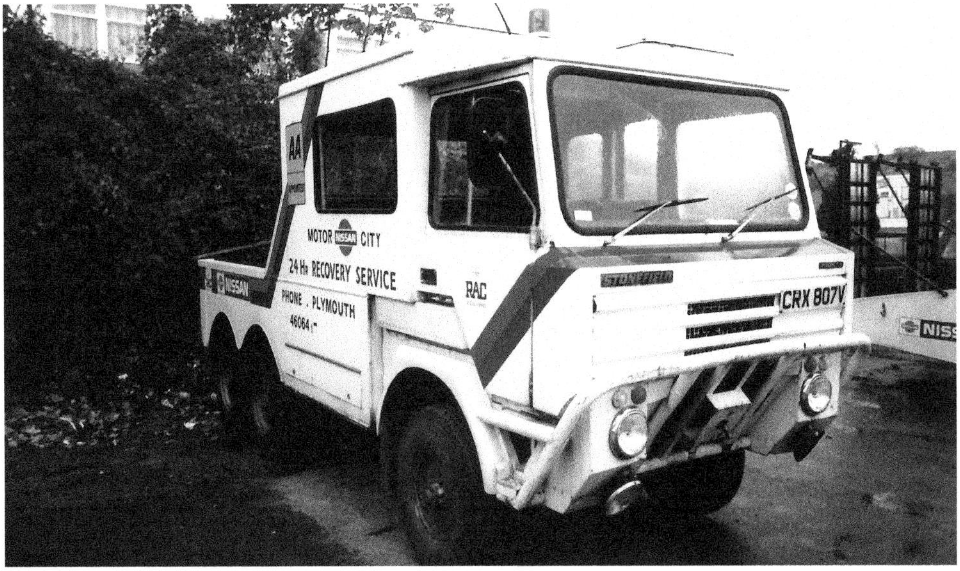

There is not much evidence of recovery equipment on this Stonefield, but it may have been removable or collapsible to allow the vehicle to be used as a pick-up truck. Stonefields were developed and built in Scotland, initially by Jim McKelvie, who introduced Volvo trucks to the UK. (P. Crang)

The attraction of something different in the fleet was not lost on some recovery operators. Weston's Recovery of Crawford, beside the M74, had this Chevrolet imported with Jerr Dan equipment. It was a great point of interest wherever it went and is seen here at a small truck show at the Whitesands in Dumfries. Its worth as a piece of equipment would be appreciated just as much.

W. H. Malcolm is the largest independent haulage company in Scotland with a large fleet of general haulage and tipper lorries. It has its own maintenance facility near Glasgow and has used a succession of recovery trucks. This Volvo was brand new when photographed, and heavily equipped to deal with whatever the fleet threw at it.

The availability of fully equipped ex-military Foden 6x6 recovery units has seen a big take up by recovery men across the country. James Gordon's fully equipped Foden is an excellent example of the type. (G. Carpenter)

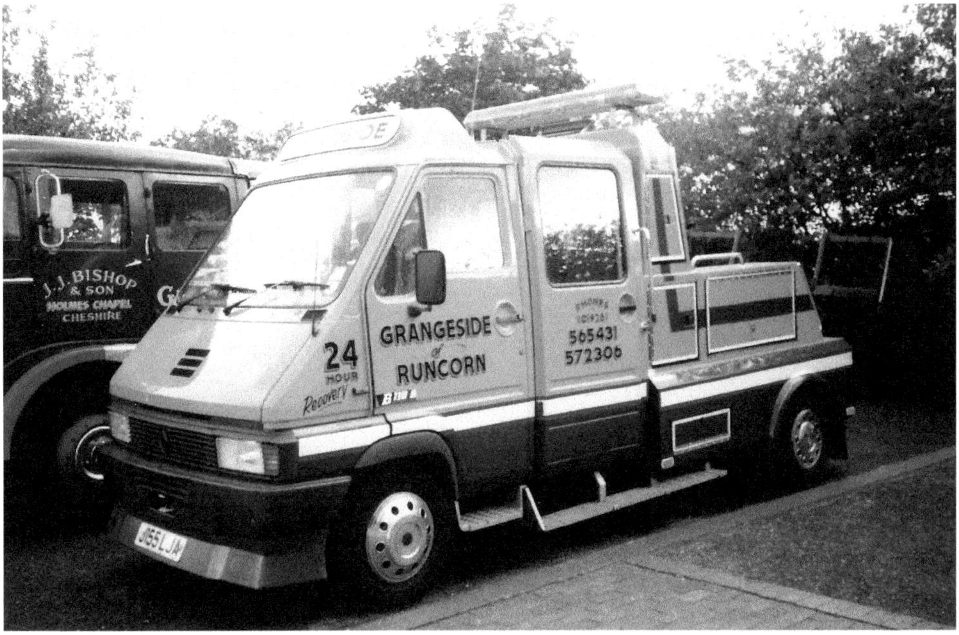

Dating from 1991, this Renault B110 is a rare example of a pure recovery truck. Most were built as slide backs and were used in car relay. This one with a double cab was operated in Merseyside, and its narrow width would have made it ideal for working in congested areas.

MTS Recovery, from Stirling, has this large DAF 95XF in its fleet. It may be the successor to the Scania 143 seen elsewhere in the book. Fitted with underlift recovery gear, it makes its presence apparent by the modern Scottish livery and prominent lettering and phone number.

A versatile vehicle in the 911 Recovery fleet is this Mercedes-Benz Unimog. With its hydraulic crane and winch, it can get to wrecked vehicles where conventional recovery types could not go.

McDougall Commercials in Dumfries has this Scania 144 with Boniface recovery equipment. With 530 bhp it would be well up to the job of heavy recovery. Note the ‘gremlin’ on the air deflector.

Another of Barry Devlin's well up to date fleet is this Volvo FM12. It has Boniface lifting gear and a tag axle with smaller wheels to spread the weight of the rear end with a suspended tow.

An impressive Mercedes-Benz Actros 1853 of 2005 in service with Hough Green Garage in Widnes. Another high-powered machine, it has Boniface lifting gear which would put it well in charge of anything it could tow. Like the Devlin Volvo, it has smaller wheels on the tag axle. (P. Crang)

We usually associate the US Freightliner marque with large-bonneted trucks in the American tradition. This small Freightliner recovery truck, like many others, may have been imported as a complete recovery truck. It works in the north-east of England.

NYR, or Neil Yates Recovery, operates an impressive fleet of recovery and haulage trucks from Maidstone, in Kent. The Kenworth shown here has a Boniface rotating crane, an extended chassis and a pusher axle. (P. Crang)

A later recovery truck used by Ian Gordon of Ayrshire was this DAF 95XF built with an underlift suitable for suspended towing of all types of large commercials. A lifting tag axle can spread the rear end weight of a suspended tow.

Another of the ex-military Foden 6x6 recovery trucks; this one is part of the JST Services fleet, which provides logging transport and port services in the west of Scotland. The winch capabilities of the Foden will be well tested in the Scottish forests.

Modern Boniface recovery equipment has become very popular and is seen fitted to the Volvo FM of Crouch Recovery. Crouch Recovery was founded in 1948 and is one of the largest recovery operators in the Midlands. It is also a dealer in ex-military vehicles.

Slades Garage in Chard, Somerset, was using this big-bonneted Scania T144 about ten years ago. It has Boniface recovery equipment and double drive rear axles. A heavily ballasted front bumper is evident. In fairly plain colours, it is nevertheless a head turner. (P. Crang)

George McPhie provides a comprehensive recovery service in the Lothians region of Scotland. His low-cabbed Mercedes-Benz Actros has Boniface recovery equipment and the small-wheeled rearmost axle regularly seen applied by this equipment manufacturer.

The rise in motoring organisations outside the AA and RAC has seen franchised recovery operators using modern types of recovery vehicles that are capable of travelling long distances. Hamilton Auto Services run this tidy Renault Master in the Green Flag livery for car and light commercial recovery. The registration number might not be age accurate, but is very appropriate.

The Westons Recovery fleet at Crawford contains this Volvo FH16. Volvo is its preferred heavyweight marque and this one is looking good in the summer sunshine outside the Weston premises, which straddle the old A74 road.

Ashley Wood Recovery operated from several depots in Dorset and Wiltshire. This five-axle Scania 144 must have been the fleet flagship when the photograph was taken about ten years ago. The rearmost axle looks to be a lifting tag type. (P. Crang)

Yet another Boniface-equipped heavy recovery truck, this DAF 95XF 480 is part of the large CMG Services Group, which has depots across the country. A very long underlift can be seen, along with the characteristic Boniface small-wheeled tag axle. (P. Crang)

One of the lighter recovery units in the 911 Recovery fleet that can be seen running around Glasgow and the west of Scotland every day is this MAN TG-L with a long wheelbase which allows light commercials to be lifted. The 911 livery is controversial in some people's opinions.

Chisholm Recovery Services operate in from Ballachulish, Inverness and Perth, which means they can be tasked to recoveries from the far north of Scotland and to the west coast islands, as well as into the Scottish Central Belt. Its DAF 95XF with Boniface equipment has just picked up a local authority Dennis refuse lorry from a layby on the A9 road. (I. Lawson)

A detailed view of an ex-military Leyland Martian recovery truck, showing the size of the vehicle and the rotating crane. The Martian was 8 feet 6 inches wide, and almost 30 feet long. This one was operated by Tom Carruthers in Dumfriesshire until he retired, when it passed to Turners of Sedgefield, in County Durham.